drift

drift

ALINE LINDEMANN

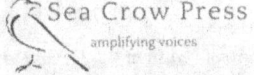
Sea Crow Press
amplifying voices

Drift
Published 2022
Sea Crow Press
ISBN: 979-8-9850080-2-9
E-ISBN: 979-8-9850080-3-6
Library of Congress Control Number: 2022933944

Cover Image by Aline Lindemann
Cover Design by Popkitty Design
Interior Design by Mary Petiet
www.seacrowpress.com
info@seacrowpress.com

for those
seeking refuge

Contents

HOME

WHITECREST BEACH

Scanning wide or scoping,
looking down, looking down, looking down,
the sea does not discriminate
the beachcomber,
revealing the same gifts
to all who meet it
toes first,
palms open.

At the shoreline,
where life grasps hands with eternity,
and footsteps sever finite
and forever lies
the exact edge of life
and death.

Do you see the boys
riding the sea— daring,
pushing, traversing
their edge?

They grab the crest
of foam and fate, the line drawn
between now and no limits,
for the risk, the risk, the risk
they say
is irrelevant.

Oh, to be them— to feel life
from within their sinewy limbs
and poppy-haired freshness.

Held here by fear
I ply a line in the sand where castoff
relics of lives passed lurk
and wait for me
to notice them.

It's enough,
perhaps.

STUCKNESS

When we find evidence
of the greater thing

out

there

somewhere

we must send a thank-you note.

It's only right.

Grace — easy.
Cue the script at every meal
(always aloud if the kids are at the table)
and sometimes silently,
depending who's around.

Blue skies, a break in traffic,
two-for-ones,
a drop in gas prices,
thank you baby Jesus
for that, too.

Gratitude — check.

And on days when greatness hides,
and doubt is a free-fall,
or we choke on treacle
others savor, filling the throat
till we're longing for death,

what do we do then?

Praying about that stuckness,
seems like a good idea,
but where

are we

to kneel?

DRIFT

You no longer
belong to me
out there beyond
the sandbar...

Quoi?
Quoi?

The gulls, the gulls,
they swoop and swoon.
Are you calling me?
I can't hear you.

The fog is rolling in and
it's harder to see you now
but you're out there, right?
You're okay?

Salt spray banishes
the lingering warmth
of your tiny hands on my cheeks –
wasn't that just yesterday?

And the flood
pushes me back
to the dune.

Quoi?
Quoi?

Are you happy, my dear?
I can't see you.

Sleek silhouette
dripping wet,
self-satisfied
and unaware that I
watch
every
move.

At last, with ease,
you traverse the surface,
smiling, sweet speck
catching your breath

suspended
on a swell.

FRAYED BITS

Steve said I should pretend
I'm going to die tomorrow.

What would you want to tell people?

Sepia-toned scraps
that look old and important,
the cap from a bottle
of Brer Rabbit molasses,
Sacred Heart medals,
frayed bits of pink linen
and orange ones too, I said

and St. Francis of Assisi,
of course.

Also,
recipes and questions for God,
books (blue ones),
seashells and purposes,
plus a cup of tea, a scissors
and a glue stick.

Steve is an astrophysicist
and he doesn't realize that we are indecisive
or, some of us are indecisive.

He doesn't understand
that many of us think in collages
or, some of us think in collages.

Or maybe, all I know for certain is that
at least one of us thinks in collages.

And she's doing just fine

most of the time.

Neap

Every time the edge of the sea retreats
it appears reluctant to do so.

Or maybe that's just me

ebbing back, back, back
to reveal stones,

smooth bits of milky white clamshell,
ochre orbs and ash gray gems

aside bones, scraps, mildew
and tangled up
funk.

BITTERSWEET

My sweet man is reclined in a deck chair,
sometimes watching me, sometimes closing his eyes,
head tilted slightly toward the sun,
which is finally out after three days of fog.

I'm wearing the t-shirt I slept in last night,
faded linen shorts, scuffed Wellies and
purple rubber gardening gloves

and I'm up to my knees in weeds —
brambly, stringy ones with Velcro-like stems,
plus bushels and tons of dandelions.

I'm even wrangling with a bit of bittersweet
which I once thought was cute —
giant clumps by the side of the road,
shoots extended willy-nilly out the top,
each one tipped with a curly q
like the swirl on a Dairy Queen soft-serve.

Learning the way of these tenacious tendrils
as they quietly obliterate every plant within reach
helped me see them as they really are —
silent killers.

But, truth be told,
and I have no reason not to be honest,
I do love a good weed-pulling sesh.
There's something therapeutic about it.
And mostly, I'm glad my husband is healing.

Two weeks post-craniotomy,
he is quiet, easily tired,
and prefers to be near me.
Though he makes steady strides,
he's unsure of himself.

So many people are praying for us.

I might have once scoffed, ever so silently,
had you told me I was in your prayers.
I thought my fortitude was enough
to push, pull and wrestle—read, research
and reason my way through.

Tender sentiment and sweet novenas were for
naïve, soft-willed ones. Sensitive types.
I couldn't think of a reason to thank you
for shooting arrows into darkness

but something has softened inside.

Bittersweet is funny.
It convinces me that I'm done tugging
because I've managed to wrap my hands
around a good, long stem to disentangle it from the
rose bush or the lilies or the holly.

But it's a fooler.
To get rid of bittersweet, I must dig deep
and trace every reach of its root,
and if it's been there a while, I might need help.
Otherwise, it will come back, leaving me bound
to repeat the struggle.

Sometimes, the tussle is gratifying, but eventually
it is no longer fulfilling nor necessary.

And eventually the hard work of eradicating
that which is deceptive creates space
for something tender and new.

HAYLEY SAYS

When I turn up the music
and paint barefoot,
who gains?

When I ruminate
over the rightness of an adverb,
who is served?

Hayley says waiting
to be more this or less that or
somehow more perfectly prepared
helps no one and

work in progress is still work.

Even awkward steps
and strokes by as imperfect
a servant as I.

AWAY

Trogir morning

A slow ripple approaches
Zoë and Grazia, docked side by side
as the golden morning light gives way
to blue haze, chrome lines and sterns.

Dong, ding-dong, ding-dong...

dear swallows, how long
have you swooped to the sounds
of bells pealing and cutting
through the cove?

Were you there when the fortress was
whole? Do you ever rest?

Charters motor in, and across the river
young men slap each other on the back
and stagger home.
One fellow trails behind
bawling last night's drinking song.

Laborers of the arch,
what did you have in mind
as you constructed
a surround for the city?

Were you there when the fortress was
whole? Did you ever rest?

How long before the swallows moved in
and the faded white flag was
raised, rippling now as
Luna Rossa
glides by?

THE STOVE MAKER

Just beyond the garden
a man crouches in the dirt
surrounded by sticks and rusted tin,

a closer look reveals his role: the stove maker.

Cooking-oil rations come in five-gallon cans
and when the oil runs out, he cuts an arch
into one side (this is where a twig fire will burn)

and twists wire into a grid —
a burner on which to place a pan.

This is what women inside the camp
use to cook food for their families,
which explains the low-hanging gray smoke
burning our eyes as we walk along aisles
of tents, careful not to trip over stones
and wobbly
strollers.

Unamuno's Tragedy

Unamuno said
truth is not always
beautiful and it is
usually not free.
Wildflowers and sunlight
are part of it, but so are black holes,
tax collectors, wayward sheep and
the walking wounded.
Addicts, lepers and prostitutes, too.
Truth is in the tragedy and
the reconciliation.
It's in the turning.

Unamuno said
faith is not a straight line.
It will not be plotted
on a growth chart or a map.
The moon and the sea
are part of it, but so are nakedness,
coarse words, wrestlers and
soiled clothes.
And the artist knows
faith is a march
through the debilitating stupor
incited by the glare of
the blank page.

Faith is
movement of the soul
toward practical truth.
Rain and shade
are part of it, but so are quack healers,
unpared apples, the breath of a friend
and an empty gaze.
Prisoners and preachers, too.
Opposed to extravagance,
opposed to despair,
Unamuno said
truth is.

PETRA

While we unloaded
boxes of clothing and food rations
women cooked over open fires,
children ran about
wearing cheap rubber slip-ons
and old men paced.

We did our best to keep up
with rambunctious young ones
while navigating anchoring ropes
draped with damp clothing.

It rained the day before our visit,
many of the tents perched
on the hillside were saturated
and there was talk of snow.

The camp was called Petra,
built on the sloped grounds
of a decrepit psychiatric asylum
near Petra of Olympus Monastery.

A girl of about ten led me by the hand
to three tents arranged around a clearing
where Yezidi women gathered
around two makeshift stoves.

An aroma of diced onions
and simmering vegetables filled my nostrils
and the women with glossy, coal black hair
and eyes of every color so stunning
that I had to concentrate on not staring
were talking and laughing with one another.

A greeting: easy smiles and generous kisses
left cheek, right cheek, and then left again.

Steps away, an older woman dressed in white,
her salt-and-pepper hair pulled into a bun
at the nape of her neck, was cleaning up.
She had just baked a batch of flatbread
by heating slabs of dough on what looked
like an overturned metal bowl
balanced over an open flame.

As I lingered, the older woman stood,
adjusted her headscarf and approached.
She wrapped her arm around my waist
and stayed close.
We shared no common language
so we stood together in silence
and watched children chase
beneath a mercury sky.

Then, she broke away,
pulled a freshly baked piece of flatbread
from her stack and handed it to me.

A thanks: I tore off small pieces
and ate one there —
lightly crisp, then warm
and chewy to the teeth —
and expressed my delight,
met with a teary-eyed smile.

I tucked the bread inside my vest,
my reverence for her gift,
said my goodbyes

and willed my teeth
not to chatter.

AEGEAN

Does the same inky blue
that slows my pulse

quicken the hearts of those who
boarded boats at the edge of the Aegean?

Do they even breathe
when they think of waves swamping
groaning rafts made for eight or ten

or when sheer numbers
made it impossible to hold on?

Would they whose loved ones
lie at the bottom
care to dip
their toes
into the inky blue
ever
again?

Can they ever be
lulled?

ON A MOUNTAINTOP

What are you, Christian?
Or... *Muslim?*
What...what *are* you,
the young Yezidi man asks, hands
folded before him on the long
wooden table where we
and a growing number of others
are gathered.

Barely a sip into a cup of tea
at the mountaintop
hotel-turned-refugee camp
where we now sit in a dimly lit
dining hall, most of the wooden chairs
upside down on their tabletops,
the expectant gazes of eight or so young men
seated shoulder to shoulder to share their stories
and to see the outsiders — the light-skinned
woman writer and the dark-skinned man
with the cameras — move in unison
from my colleague's face to mine.

Our inquirer's angular eyebrows peak into
thick straight hair combed smooth
and straight back from his low forehead
and a short list of options fires
through my mind.

This particular trip,
and years of research preceding it,
were so enriched by the attentiveness
of our newest Yezidi friends,
our escorts to this remote mountaintop,
eager to share their stories,
deflect light from my colleague's photo shoots
or huddle with us under a dilapidated
umbrella waiting for rain to pass.

With the wrong answer, their trust
in us and in our dedication to their plight
could vaporize.

Plus, it took us forever to get here
along winding roads above clouds,
past herds of rangy, lumbering cows
and at least 40 minutes away
from the nearest gas station, food market
or medical provider, to meet the families
that could not be accommodated
with the rest of their community in Serres.

My colleague, by his own admission
not a super devout Muslim, might not be
so warmly welcomed by displaced people
forced to survive 74 genocides over thousands of years
perpetrated by people who also call themselves Muslim,
the most recent of which resulted in the murder
and kidnapping of 10,000 Yazidis,
including hundreds of boys destined
for transformation into ISIS soldiers
and the enslavement of 3000 women
and girls considered sabaya—spoils of war.

Islam has been poorly represented
in Yezidi communities.

Exposing a silver cross hanging on a chain
that has fallen behind the collar of my t-shirt,
I hold the eyes of the young man.

He nods,
and I change the subject.

Hadi Said

I decide who I am, said Hadi
and him saying this is a smooth stone
that I turn in my palm.

He is Yezidi
and he knows things.

Verily I say that
divinity lives in nature
and sacred energy courses
right through us.

I know things, too.

If doctrine is a stone, precious and true
and sacredness is water upon my forehead,
then divinity is dried up dune grass blowing
beyond my reach, crab shells lying askew,
jaunty driftwood emerging from tall reeds
in less-tread places, and a gull dropping
a clam on a craggy rock from ever greater
heights until at last, it shatters
and dinner is served
to chicks
waiting
in the
nest.

Their calls
Hadi's words
sand slipping
along the sandy path

my creed.

RETURN TO ATHENS

Semi-reclined in an upholstered chair
in the hotel lobby sipping coffee,
my travel mate looks well rested.

Another cup, a freshen up,
a cab hailed and we set off for Skaramangas.

Are we sure we want to go there?
our driver wants to know,

surely we are mistaken?

Most visitors to Athens
aren't interested in visiting
a commercial shipyard.

Past massive cranes and dinosaur-sized
erector sets surrounding concrete warehouses
with yellowing plastic window panels

our driver leaves us and we have no idea
how we'll get back to the city.

For now, we keep pace
with the trickle of people
most wearing long sleeves and head scarves
treading beyond the rusted wreckage
toward a gap in the chain-link fence
at the end of the dirt road.

They live here. They know the way.

We stroll through the gate like
we know exactly where we're headed
and don't dare look back for fear
of getting stopped
by gray-clad guards
catching
our eyes.

HOME AGAIN

WRACK

Shuffling along at high tide
as froth edges near
is useful when you have a knot
inside refusing to unravel.

Uncontained holiness lures you
along beach path softness
and the shh shh of the reeds tells truths,

as do exposed ribs of a dolphin carcass.

Gulls ride an updraft
and silver glints across the surface
of freshly wetted sand at the shoreline
but the wrack is where death
leaves beauty behind.

Purple grooves of a mussel shell
turned over reveal ivory pearlessence
and tawny stacked ridges
of a whelk egg case curl askew
in withered eel grass.

Sometimes you're in
and sometimes you're cast aside.
Sometimes you reach and connect and it's divine,
other times you're tucked in and untouched.

And sometimes you're just
a chalky old moon snail

standing alone.

THE CONFUSING TIME

The notes you heed are choirs of the past
but there's no reverence here, dear
for hymns irrelevant

so banish the copycats
and scrape away the mess
but send them away kindly — tenderly

for they are learning, too.

This is the confusing time
and there is a certain way
that things should go—
you know, things

and this way — it's not normal.

So if you're given thirty pieces
just shake your little fist
if you like and then

slice some space
right down the center
and say thank you — politely
as you exit and let
the draft blow thru.

The heart — your heart — will shudder
just a bit when you realize
you can't see the other side
and that's how you will know

you are alive.

MOTH

So much light
behind you and
on all sides but you don't see

your own halo.

You hug your little arms sending
warmth back to the core
of your chest deep inside

because it's hard to
make sense of a washing glow
what with the
flit, flit, plip and plip

of that moth against the window,

poor thing.

Do you pity the little one
on the outside
just craving that light

inside?

Do you love her?

SOUL PASS

Flittering lines of apparent
unimportance snap
through my brain too quickly
to seize any sense of cause or effect,

foot steps, bird shrieks
glint and glimmer of sunlight
off someone's living room window,
another bird, call button, another bird,
gravel slip, breathing tube,
beige linoleum, pant pant pant.

I have trudged and puffed
over the crest of this craggy mountain,
I know these rocky hills.
When the sun ekes over the boulder
at the bend in the path, the glare and
shadows will keep my time.

Hitting a familiar dip in the road where
a coyote once stared me down,
a cool breeze wafts past me,
through me.

I never sensed that wisp before,
certainly not on a July day in the desert.
Was it you, at last released
from pumps and forced air?

Mesquite

Cast shadows travel and weave
across matted earth
while I float and swing
sunk in a netted sling
suspended from a
charred mesquite tree.

Black straps wrap and buckles cinch
around strained limbs and
knotted fingers clawing at
blue sky that hold me
sans judgement, stretch
without complaint.

Beetles emerge from
a tarry crevasse and
rough bark splays over a bulge
at the bend where
the dark trunk
and rough-hewn skin
splits and splinters

but at least
I am
held.

SADDLE STITCHED

saddle stitches

shroud hopes of
the sensitive one,

lay threadbare
the nerves
of the unruly one,

bind burdens
too grotesque
for daylight,

hem and hide
knotted truths
and sensitivities,

shroud rash dreams
and unsung envy

and do their best
to heal the wounds

TRAIL

I left last March
which was some months ago (I lost count)
and I thought I'd only be away
a few days.

Receipts, a mammogram reminder,
and the phone number for a dog shelter
scribbled on the back of a coupon
for a free taco remained in a basket
of things to be sorted later
and now it's much later
and I don't recognize
this trail from another time.

It's a lot of work being alive.

Simplicity is so praised these days
but the lives we carve
are meant for appendages, aren't they?
How else can we reach out
and touch one another?
How else might I embrace the orphan, the
widow, the prisoner
or the sweet pup left to die?

Love — the hearty kind — serves
and doing that well requires some things.

But rebirthed into this space —
into the desert
watching trees,
noticing stones and the sky
is enough
for now.

Resources

To learn more about needs of refugees, visit

Lifting Hands International
liftinghandsinternational.org

Carry the Future
carrythefuture.org

The Welcome to America Project
wtap.org

International Rescue Committee
rescue.org

About the Author

Aline Lindemann is an artist and writer whose work honors and explores the intersection of spirituality and nature with a special emphasis on the meaning of home. Though she has traveled far and wide both for pleasure and in service to nonprofits that provide for displaced people seeking refuge in unfamiliar lands, it is her beloved Cape Cod home and an unceasing fascination with the sea that inspire and pervade her art and her writing.

ABOUT THE PRESS

Sea Crow Press is committed to amplifying voices that might otherwise go unheard with a focus on positive change and great storytelling. Founded in 2020, the growing press is home to an eclectic collection of creative nonfiction, fiction, and poetry. At Sea Crow Press we believe the small press plays an essential part in contemporary arts by amplifying its voices. Sea Crow Press is committed to building an accessible community of writers and dedicated to telling stories that matter.

www.ingramcontent.com/pod-product-compliance
Lightning Source LLC
Chambersburg PA
CBHW011231120626
46549CB00008B/3234